Road to Victory

D–Day, June 1944 to VJ Day, August 1945

Classic, Rare and Unseen Photographs
from the

Road to Victory

D–Day, June 1944 to VJ Day, August 1945

James Alexander

**Trans
Atlantic
Press**

Published by Transatlantic Press in 2010

Transatlantic Press
38 Copthorne Road
Croxley Green
Hertfordshire, WD3 4AQ, UK

Photographs © *Daily Mail Archive*
© Transatlantic Press 2010

A catalogue record for this book is available
from the British Library.

ISBN 978–1–907176–22–7
Printed in China

War throughout the world

You ask, what is our aim? I can answer with one word: Victory—victory at all costs, victory in spite of all terror, victory however long and hard the road may be.

Given the circumstances of Britain's isolated stand against a Nazi-dominated 'fortress' Europe, these words of British Prime Minister, Winston Churchill's 1940 speech to Parliament might have sounded unrealistic to the point of delusion. The US Government was certainly sceptical until, in the summer and autumn of 1940, against all odds, Britain's aircraft and ground defences repelled the German attacks in the Battle of Britain, set as an overture to 'Operation Sealion' – the planned Nazi invasion of mainland Britain. Despite this significant success, Britain, supported by her Commonwealth Allies, faced a momentous struggle to survive under constant threat of aerial bombardment and attacks on vital shipping. Even with the entry of USSR on Britain's side in June 1941, the road to victory remained difficult. However, once the US entered the war in December 1941 after a shock Japanese attack on the US fleet, the final result was more predictable, though the cost and timescale would be less certain.

World War II was different in so many ways from any other conflict preceding it, not just in sheer scale, but in the intense ideological dynamics that fuelled the war machines of two of the principal belligerents: the Axis powers of Germany and Japan believed that domination of the defeated enemy meant total victory and that there was no alternative to victory other than death – for them, their military forces and their civilian populations. The other main distinction was the rise of modern warfare based on swift moving, powerfully armed forces – on land, sea and in the air. Germany and Japan seemed to grasp this in advance of their opponents, with the Nazi Blitzkrieg in Western Europe and Japan's pre-emptive air strike on Pearl Harbor followed by rapid deployment through the Pacific. However, the obsessive ideologies that achieved early victories against the ill-prepared Allies, would ultimately lead to the failure of their regimes, as both Germany and Japan expended their people and material to the point of exhaustion. The USSR, fighting on the side of the Allies, expended itself in the same way as Germany and Japan, but from an almost endless supply of manpower and production.

Hitler's second shock after the failure of the Battle of Britain and the cancelling of 'Operation Sealion', was the Afrika Korp's defeat by the Allies in the Western Desert, beginning with General Bernard Law Montgomery's rout in the famous Battle of El Alamein in October 1942. Churchill famously described this significant victory as 'not the end, it is not even the beginning of the end. But it is, perhaps, the end of the beginning', acknowledging it as an important turning point on the road to final victory.

Thus, when Churchill met with Roosevelt and De Gaulle in Casablanca in January 1943, discussions turned to the invasion of Italy, now that the Axis grip on the Mediterranean had been loosened by the North Africa victory, and ultimately the complete overthrow of the Nazis. By May of that year the Allies had completed their North Africa campaign by capturing more than 250,000 German and Italian troops. This paved the way for Allied landings in Italy in September 1943 which resulted in Italy's official surrender. However, Italy fought on under German subjugation and the road to final victory here was to be at the expense of many ferocious battles with significant casualties on all sides.

Nevertheless, the success in Italy resulted in plans for an Allied counter-attack against Nazi Germany. US General Dwight D Eisenhower – 'Ike' – was named as Supreme Allied Commander Europe in December 1943 to lead this daring attack. Britain's General Montgomery was appointed to command all Allied land forces in Europe and in January 1944, the Supreme Headquarters Allied Expeditionary Force (SHAEF) set up its base in Bushy Park, west of London: preparations for D-Day had begun in earnest.

The key to the success of 'Operation Overlord' was to be surprise, speed and overwhelming force. The German OKW, or High Command, made an assumption – which the Allies encouraged – that the invasion of France would take place in the Pas de Calais region. While this was logical, the Germans failed to realise that the Allies' naval superiority gave them confidence to take the longer route to Normandy's shelving sandy beaches, which had been carefully surveyed in the planning phase. Key factors in landing would be the tides and the weather, giving a strict window of opportunity; initial plans were set for May 1944, later changed to June.

During the build-up to invasion, Britain became a giant military camp with Allied troops billeted in camps and private houses around the country, but concentrated around the south coast of England. Civilians were banned from the coast and great pains were taken to maintain the deception to the Germans that the invasion would take place in the Pas de Calais, including dummy installations in southeast England to fool aerial reconnaissance. Compromised Nazi intelligence agents fed back reports given to them by their Allied masters. Finally, as part of 'Operation Fortitude', a dead British officer was planted on the shores of Spain carrying a set of invasion plans for Pas de Calais.

The Normandy Landings were planned in great detail but even at this early phase casualties were not avoided. One of the biggest rehearsals for 'Operation Overlord' was 'Exercise Tiger', a training exercise in Lyme Bay in which around 700 US personnel died when German E-Boats were alerted and torpedoed the training troop carriers. Men who made it to the beach then failed to keep within marked boundaries and were killed in friendly fire. Setbacks like this were kept very secret to maintain morale.

To meet the logistical challenge of beach landings, specially adapted craft were constructed, some of which had already seen service in the Pacific. As the Allies would not have control of the ports in Northern France and the beaches on which the landings were to take place would not have deep anchorage, the Mulberry Harbour was created – a collection of floating quays to be towed to just off Omaha beach and ballasted to the seabed, enabling materials to be unloaded from ship to shore.

The combined air and sea landings began in the early hours of 6 June 1944, with British and US airborne forces parachuting and gliding to secure key inland objectives. The largest seaborne invasion force in history set out from assembly points all around the southern coast of Britain: some troop-carrying landing craft, like the DUKW, had to be loaded with troops just offshore from the beaches – bigger landing craft sailed across the English Channel already loaded – a miserable experience for the troops on board as these shallow-draft vessels were not designed for open sea. Nevertheless, the preparations for D-Day gave successful results in most cases, with American forces landing on Omaha and Utah beaches in the west, adjacent to the Cotentin peninsula; British and Canadian forces landed on Gold, Juno and Sword beaches to the east.

Despite the complete surprise achieved by the Allied landings, German resistance was strong, particularly from a Waffen SS Panzer Division that was recuperating in the area before going back to active service. This succeeded in holding back the planned speed of the Allied advance and it would not be until 18 July that the Allied forces were able to break out from the Normandy coast beachhead in 'Operation Cobra', with General Patton striking into Brittany and Montgomery's 21st Army group heading into Belgium towards the Rhine.

Once the breakout from Normandy had been achieved, more bloodily fought objectives were gained, culminating in the liberation of Paris on 25 August. By this time, the Germans were suffering on the Italian and Mediterranean fronts with the liberation of Rome on 5 June and 'Operation Dragoon' reclaiming southern France from 15 August. On the Eastern front they were subject to massive and fast moving attacks by the Red Army's 'Operation Bagration', launched on 22 June. Even the Furher himself had come under attack: Hitler had come close to death on 20 July in the assassination plot led by Colonel Claus von Stauffenberg. Additionally, in the Pacific theatre, things were not going well for Germany's ally, Japan. The Pacific Fleet, under US command, won a decisive sea battle against the Japanese in the Philippine Sea and the Marianas Islands were reclaimed – providing a strategic base for US Air Forces to bomb Japan.

Allied Supreme Command knew that Germany would be defeated; Eisenhower's 'broad front' strategy in the West used superior Allied forces against the stretched Wehrmacht which had to fight battlefronts in the east and south. Eisenhower's most talented Generals – Patton and Montgomery – favoured short sharp action with a view to bringing Germany to its knees as soon as possible. Patton, in France, was consistent in his rapid tactics; Montgomery, in the lowlands of Belgium, wanted a strategic strike, which he thought would break the back of German opposition: he persuaded Eisenhower to back 'Operation Market Garden', a highly ambitious combined operation using airborne troops and fast-moving armour that should have secured a route for Allied Forces directly to the German border, crossing the River Rhine at Arnhem. This brave and inspired attempt, launched in mid-September, foundered. The plan failed at many basic levels, but above all it under-estimated the will

of German troops to fight, and as a result many thousands of Allied soldiers became casualties or were taken prisoner.

The failure of 'Operation Market Garden' stalled the Allied advance in the Lowlands and in December the advancing southern Allied spearhead under Patton met stiff resistance at the city of Metz at France's border with Germany; it was heavily fortified and again the advance slowed. The change of pace in the Western Front and the influx of hardened German troops from the Lowlands gave Hitler the opportunity of mustering his forces. In a replay of the original Blitzkrieg that took the Lowlands and laid France open, Hitler instructed a daring counter-attack through the Ardennes which would recapture Antwerp and bisect the Allied armies. Counting on surprise, speed and an enemy made sluggish by winter weather, the Germans advanced on 15 December 1944, beginning the terrible month-long Battle of the Bulge. Allied Forces, occupying an area of little strategic importance, were taken completely by surprise; the quality of the Allied troops was mixed but the battle-hardened 101st Airborne held back the German attack on Bastogne, a strategic target for the success of their plan. The brief surge into the Allied occupied territory created a salient, which, instead of becoming the corridor to Antwerp, simply acted as a deadly cul-de-sac.

Despite the ultimate defeat of the German Ardennes offensive, the Allies realised they were still facing a determined and resourceful enemy. Although Germany was being systematically destroyed by strategic bombing, the Allies could not calculate the remaining Wehrmacht strength, as military intelligence coming out of Germany

was very limited. However, the Battle of the Bulge had exhausted Germany's remaining reserves and finished off the Luftwaffe – although V1 and V2 rockets continued to be effective weapons and the latest Messerschmitt Me262 jet fighters continued to give an impression of strength.

As the winter weather cleared on the Western Front, the Allies pressed home their advantage and crossed the Rhine in March 1945, heading steadily for Berlin and taking many prisoners on their way. Gruesome discoveries were made by the advancing troops as they liberated prisoner of war camps and, worse, the Nazi death camps. In the east, the Russians hastened towards Berlin, meeting their western allies at Turgau on the River Elbe on 24 April. Berlin was now encircled and by the end of the month Hitler had committed suicide; his remaining generals agreed an unconditional surrender on 7 May, which was celebrated as VE Day (Victory in Europe Day) around the world on 8 May. Berlin lay in ruins, along with many of the major cities of Europe, but a terrible chapter was at last closed.

Churchill's VE Day speech reminded the world of the urgent task of defeating Japan; the steady advance of Allied forces in the Pacific – on the mainland through Burma and across the ocean through the Philippines and other islands – kept its impetus, despite determined and often suicidal defence by the Japanese. The taking of the island of Iwo Jima in March 1945 had signalled the final phase of the Pacific war, but there was no sign that the Japanese resolve was weakening: on Iwo Jima almost the entire Japanese garrison perished in its defence, a scenario repeated on other islands. At sea, Allied naval ships were subject to continuous Kamikaze raids, but these could not deter the advance to Japan which, in spring 1945, suffered heavy strategic bombing.

On 21 June, the island of Okinawa fell, surrendering territory that was Japanese homeland. But the bitter fighting continued. Allied leaders met up on 17 July for the famous Potsdam Conference outside Berlin: Harry S Truman, who had stepped into the presidential role following the unexpected death of Roosevelt in April 1944, met Stalin for the first time and enraged the Russian leader by holding back information on the top-secret Manhattan project that was building the nuclear bomb. The Potsdam Declaration gave an ultimatum to Japan to surrender or be destroyed; together, Truman and Churchill had decided that the atomic bomb would be dropped on Japan if it did not comply. This British commitment stood, even though Churchill had to step down during the Conference to be replaced by Clement Attlee, the new British Prime Minister.

The Japanese simply ignored the Potsdam Declaration: they interpreted the terms of the Declaration as taking away their Imperial powers and submitting their leaders to be tried for War Crimes. The die was cast and on 6 August the world changed forever when the first nuclear device was dropped on Hiroshima killing tens of thousands, flattening the city and creating national confusion – but no surrender. The bombing of Nagasaki followed three days later. With some further delaying tactics, the Emperor announced to his people that Japan would surrender, because to do otherwise would result in total annihilation. On 15 August, Japan capitulated: finally the world could begin a recovery process that would take years and generations. On VJ Day, jubilant crowds in the Allies' cities around the world began celebrations that would continue in some form or another for over a year, ranging from street parties to victory parades.

The road to victory had indeed been hard; the road to a lasting peace would not be easy and had to be planned for. Thus, in the second half of 1944, a series of discussions between Allied leaders had taken place at a country mansion called Dumbarton Oaks near Washington DC. The Dumbarton Oaks Conference planned for the future stability of Europe after the Allied victory, seeking a guaranteed, lasting peace so that another cataclysm should not shatter the world. The nascent United Nations took form and its charter took effect on 24 October 1945: governments of the world were determined that a global war would never be repeated.

Road to Victory presents a detailed pictorial history of the last 14 months of the Second World War, capturing scenes of battle in the varied theatres across the globe where the endgame was played out. The spectacular photographs from the *Daily Mail* archive reveal at first-hand what soldiers and civilians faced in history's most terrible conflict.

D-Day rehearsal

Above: Operation Overlord was planned with the utmost secrecy to ensure that the German Command would continue to believe that the logical Allied invasion point would be the Pas de Calais area. Amazingly the secret was kept even though the whole of Britain effectively became a transit and training camp for the forthcoming landings. The massed troops underwent training to prepare them for the landings. The most notorious, Operation Tiger, set out to create realistic conditions for the 30,000 participating troops in the last week of April 1944. In nine troop ships, the US forces were to land on Slapton Sands in Devon where similar geography and terrain to their Normandy objectives were found. The convoy was intercepted by German E-boats and in the ensuing attack three transports were damaged or sunk, taking over 500 lives. Further misfortune hit over 300 more troops who made it to the beach but ignored important markers, and walked into a friendly fire zone. SHAEF Commander Eisenhower had decided his men should be exposed to the most lifelike enactment and a British heavy cruiser provided a barrage on the coastline with live ammunition as the men beached. In total, 749 soldiers and 197 US Navy personnel were killed. The tragic loss of these men was kept secret for several months and the names released with the casualties of D-Day.

Above: A DUKW amphibious troop carrier, known to all as 'Duck' boards a Tank Landing Ship or LST. American designed and built, based on a GM truck and engine, the craft could transport over water and land. Heavy duty pumps would keep the craft afloat when holed by gunfire and the driver could alter the air pressure in the tyres whilst driving, allowing the vehicle to negotiate soft sand and mud or normal road surface. Over 2,000 DUKWs were supplied to Britain under the US Lend-Lease programme; the name looks like an acronym but it is just GM's coding for the vehicle's specifications.

Ike encourages 101st Airborne

Above: General Dwight D Eisenhower talks with paratroopers of the 101st Airborne Division on 5 June prior to embarking on their spearhead mission that would successfully secure strategic positions just beyond the Omaha beachhead in the early hours of D-Day. The original photographs released by the censor required the 101st's Screaming Eagle insignia to be blanked out for publication. The 101st served throughout the European campaign and took an important role in Operation Market Garden and the Battle of the Bulge.

Opposite: Loading the landing craft required great care: although designed for the invasion and adapted for the shallow Normandy beaches, these were little more than modified barges so their load distribution was critical. A similar design was used for different purposes: seen here are Landing Craft Tank, the heavy version which would carry tanks as well as the half-tracks and trucks pictured. 1,500 were built in the USA, many of them far inland, floated downstream to the coast and then transshipped to Britain where some 900 were manufactured locally. These heavily laden craft crossed the English channel under their own power, setting out from concealed positions in ports and estuaries along Britain's south coast.

The greatest armada of all time

Above: US Infantry attacked on Omaha and Utah beaches next to the Cherbourg peninsula; aboard their landing craft they are about to beach. Shells are bursting on the shore from a naval barrage but the men look calm, protected by the armoured ramp down which they will soon run to meet the enemy. These craft carried a platoon - around 30 men - possibly a jeep and, apart from the armour at the front, were mainly constructed in plywood to a design by a US timber merchant called Andrew

Higgins; they were known as 'Higgins Boats'. Eisenhower said that without them the Allies would not have won the war.

Opposite: 5,000 ships, manned by nearly 200,000 naval personnel, made this the largest invasion armada of all time and on the fiirst day more than 175,000 troops were transported along with their armament, transport and supplies.

In sight of the shore

Above: The landings were no party for the infantry. They had to descend into landing craft down rope nets from their troop ships and in many instances wade ashore under fire - all with their full equipment. Here British troops are about to join their welcoming party of heavy armour already occupying the beachhead.

Opposite: British troops were designated to take Gold, Juno and Sword beaches; here on Sword, near the port of Ouistreham they form up to march towards Caen. Arromanches and Courseulles were the towns near Juno and Sword.

Wading to land

Above: This picture shows well the broad shelving beaches selected for the Normandy landings. While they offered easier landings to the Allied forces they also offered deadly sweep of fire for defenders. The landings were prepared with extraordinary care, including geological surveys months before the invasion - made by British mini submarines. If the Germans had in any way expected the Allied landings the slaughter would have been horrific. The low tide on 6 June allowed the beaches to be cleared of mines and other obstacles, nonetheless the outcome was laden with risk. Reportedly, Eisenhower carried with him a speech prepared in the event of the landings' failure.

Opposite: Heavily laden GIs wade ashore where half-tracks wait to help with their loads and give a shield in the first vulnerable moments ashore. In the distance a file of troops heads inland.

A constant stream of supplies

Above: After the initial onslaught, the flood of men and material continued for weeks with the Mulberry floating harbours giving moorings and protection for the supply ships. Around 600,000 military personnel would come ashore on Omaha beach as the Allied forces set about the business of reclaiming Europe.

Opposite: A barrage balloon floats over this bustling beachhead. On the distant ridge can be seen the hospital tents marked with red crosses. Thanks to intensive RAF Bomber Command activity during the run up to D-Day, the Luftwaffe was more or less neutralised, with airfields destroyed and radar knocked out. Targets were chosen with care - focus given to the Pas de Calais while systematically destroying the rail infrastructure across northern France. Under this 'smokescreen', a key gun emplacement covering Utah and Omaha beaches was bombed out by 52 RAF Lancaster planes.

Moment of surrender

Above: Allied troops met different levels of resistance; this US paratrooper, armed to the teeth, holds a terrified German prisoner at bayonet point. German intelligence relating to the Allied invasion was fragmented to say the least. German Panzer units near the invasion zone delayed engagement because only Hitler could command them into action: the Fuhrer's aides dared not waken him from sleep with news of the invasion.

Opposite: French villagers look on dispassionately as German prisoners under escort are marched to prison camps at the coast.

Stretcher party

Above: Eight days after D-Day, captured Germans carry one of their wounded fellows by stretcher to the waiting troop ships which would ferry prisoners to detention camps in Britain. One young soldier holds on to a precious ration tin.

Opposite: US troops converge in this liberated French village four days after D-Day where the *tricolore* is restored to its rightful place at the *mairie*. A DUKW blocks the road while Military Police guard two wounded German prisoners in the jeep transporting them to a prison camp.

Captured sniper

Right: The town of Ste Mere Eglise was the first French settlement to be liberated in fierce fighting by airborne troops; this German sniper captured there may be getting a comfortable ride but he's also in the firing line should his compatriots decide to attack the jeep armed with a heavy machine gun.

Opposite: The port of Isigny stood just outside the line set as the D-Day front line objective. Although tiny, its wharves, used for transporting the famed local dairy produce, would prove useful for offloading Allied supplies. In hard fighting, the town was bombarded in the early days of invasion, destroying around 60% of its buildings as can be seen from the main street pictured here.

Evacuees find safety

In the days following D-Day the town of Pont l'Abbé was fiercely defended by German troops who also fought every hedgerow and sunken lane between the town and advancing US forces. Eventually a massive bombardment wiped out the town on 12 June and the Germans moved out. French families, with a few possessions, flee their destroyed homes and try to avert their eyes from the horrors around them.

Opposite: The threat of Nazi invasion and the devastation of the Blitz might have subsided but the people of Britain suffered a new assault as the first V1 bomb landed on London on 13 June. Evacuation of civilians continued. Here some of the 400 evacuees moved into Prestwich in Greater Manchester, are helped out by a friendly 'clippie' and an ARP officer.

Misburg refinery attacked

The scale of Allied bombing over Europe became immense. On 20 June alone, the US 8th Air Force sent out over 1,500 bombers with fighter escorts to attack strategic targets. 191 B 24 Liberators were directed to the Misburg oil refinery near Hanover, pictured here billowing smoke following the raid, when 169 planes dropped high explosive bombs in a daylight raid.

Opposite: Nearly 400 US 8th Air Force B-17 bombers hit Hamburg on 18 June; it would not be the last raid but already the port city was devastated as this photograph of Moeneckeburg Strasse, a prominent business street, shows. The strategic bombing of German cities at this stage of the war would be hotly debated in years to come, but this was not yet the height of the terrible destruction wrought from the air by Allied forces.

Destruction of Caen

One of Normandy's principal cities and strategically placed for road and river transport, Caen suffered a terrible fate in the aftermath of D-Day; Montgomery had set its early liberation as a priority target but an unexpected German Panzer counterattack halted the British spearhead and it was not until 7 July that Canadian forces entered Caen after it was heavily bombarded. Over 1,000 civilians died before the final liberation on 18 July. Here a Curé walks among the ruins; Caen's historic cathedral and university were both destroyed in the Allied assault.

Opposite: Captured German troops were marshalled on Omaha beach to be transported to prison camps in Britain. The two young soldiers seen here claim to be 18 but are obviously just boys. This photograph provided evidence to the British public that Germany was running short of manpower.

Pensive prisoner

Right: The war is over for this German officer who displays his Iron Cross and Infantry Assault Badge. He was captured after the successful completion of the three-week campaign to secure the Cotentin Peninsula and its most important prize, the port of Cherbourg which was extensively sabotaged by the defending Nazis.

Opposite: As Operation Overlord pushed forwards in Western France, breaking out from the Normandy Bocage from 18 July, Allied Forces marched steadily northwards in Italy, liberating Rome on 4 June; the capture of the strategic Adriatic port of Ancona on the same day as the Normandy breakout, marked the inevitable collapse of Northern Italy; here in the Piedmont, a German soldier waves a white flag of surrender from his foxhole.

Flushed out

Above: Moments later, the soldier emerges to be captured by Polish troops who figured prominently in the Italian campaign. A substantial number of Allied troops, mainly American and French, were taken out of the Italian campaign in summer 1944 to support Operation Dragoon - the invasion of Southern France from the Mediterranean.

Opposite: In the ruins of Carentan at the base of the Cotentin Peninsula, firemen clear rubble after the liberation of the town by US forces. Field Marshal Erwin Rommel instructed the German defenders of Carentan to fight to the last man and the battle was bitterly fought in close combat.

Advancing through Italy

Above: French troops man this anti-tank unit as it rolls through Bolsena in Italy around the time of Operation Overlord. The M3 half-track tows an M3 37mm gun that was no match for the legendary German 88 anti-tank gun, which had four times the range and much heavier ammunition.

Opposite: The German garrison at Cherbourg numbered over 20,000 and had nowhere to go, cut off by the advancing American troops. Defeat was inevitable but their demolition squads rendered the port unusable until mid-August. The last defenders were silenced on 1 July and the captured troops were marched to the Omaha beachhead.

Capturing the Marianas

Left: On 2 July, US paratroopers descend to their LZ on Noemfoor Island, a Japanese stronghold with three airstrips. Its strategic position could give defensive support to the occupied Marianas Islands, which were a major objective of the US campaign in the Pacific and the Philippines. These airborne troops were reinforcements for the ground forces that had already taken the island. The airfields would be used for strategic strikes, contributing to the liberation of the Philippines, around 800 miles away.

Opposite: The unmistakable figure of General Charles de Gaulle, pictured as he lands on the Normandy beachhead eight days after D-Day. Leader of the Free French government in exile and future President of France, de Gaulle was the incarnation of the French people to the US and British political leaders who viewed the French capitulation and then Vichy cooperation with the Nazi regime as deeply lacking. Churchill was relieved after Dunkirk that Britain no longer had to take responsibility for its ally. De Gaulle once notably said 'France has no friends, only interests'. His stalwart protection of those interests isolated him among the Allied leaders.

Bayeux liberation

Left and Opposite: Scenes captured in Bayeux as the town, one of the first to be liberated on 7 June, celebrates Bastille Day, 14 July. This day, this occasion in this place was very symbolic and the biggest crowd ever seen in the town assembled, comprising local citizens, Allied troops, French Resistance fighters and many refugees from the vicinity, particularly Caen which had over 35,000 homeless.

Sunday Mass

Above: The settlement of Colombelles east of Caen was the location of a steelworks which was heavily fortified by German troops. On 18 July Bomber Command made a daylight raid on the installation, reducing it to ruins and forcing the defendants to abandon their position. Three captured German soldiers are marched to detention.

Opposite: On a quiet Sunday morning, inhabitants of Creully make their way to Mass passing by the town's monument to the dead of World War I. They are joined by British and US troops. No doubt a few kilometres distant, a similar situation would be taking place only with German soldiers observing their Christian duties.

Hitlerjugend SS

Left: The insignia on this 18-year-old wounded German soldier shows him to be Waffen SS. The recently formed 12 SS Panzer Division was composed of Hitler Youth born in 1926 and led by veteran officers. The division was newly activated in Normandy and engaged the Allied invaders from 7 June with enduring ferocity. A regimental commander, Kurt Meyer, was tried for War Crimes, convicted of massacring 140 captured Canadian troops early in the fighting.

Opposite: In the late stages of the Allied breakout from Normandy, code-named Operation Cobra, US forces under George Patton captured the coastal town of Avranches, the gateway to Brittany. After a massive aerial bombardment and an irresistible armoured advance, Germans fled their strategic defensive positions, some of them even crossing the dangerous sands of the bay to reach Mont St Michel. Despite a fierce counterattack, the liberation of Avranches on 31 July held, allowing a rapid advance to Le Mans. Many Germans were trapped and surrendered - here a column of 2,000 prisoners is escorted by US troops.

Battle of Falaise Gap

Above: A knocked-out German tank burns after being bulldozed off the highway. Following the breakout from the beachhead, Allied forces began an encircling movement to trap the German armies in the area of Normandy centred on the town of Falaise. The Battle of Falaise Gap was a pivotal conflict, whereby German forces, instructed to hold their position and resist the overwhelming Allied offensive, knew they were about to be surrounded but fought desperately to keep an avenue of escape. On 21 August, the Allies finally closed the gap, trapping an estimated 50,000 Germans and leaving a clear path to Paris which was liberated on 25 August.

Opposite: Patton's headlong advance south and west liberated Britanny's capital, Rennes, on 4 August. The city controlled transport routes essential for Axis communications in Brittany. The retreating Germans blew up the bridges of the city as they left. Following their liberation of Rennes, the Americans constructed four prison camps that housed 50,000 captured German troops; at that time the population of Rennes was only about 100,000 people.

Berlin bombed

Above: In a well-executed campaign, Operation Dragoon gained a beachhead on a 100-mile-long strip of the Mediterranean coast near Marseille on 15 August. Paratroopers and glider-borne units took inland targets while combined US and French Allied forces attacked from the sea, landing over 90,000 men in the first day of battle. The liberation of Marseille gave the southern Allied armies the benefit of a strategic port, which, combined with a restored rail network, would give a supply chain directly into Germany from France - invaluable in the days to come.

Opposite: Allied airpower maintained a busy tactical and strategic schedule during the summer of 1944, destroying German production facilities, oil storage depots, railways, bridges and airfields around France and across Germany from the Baltic south; after Operation Dragoon, airbases in the South of France provided another line of attack. Here bombs are photographed dropping on Berlin - some believed to have damaged Hitler's Chancellery. In fact Berlin received little serious attention during the summer and it would not be until 1945 that strategic bombing of the capital would recommence.

MENU *5
FIRST HALF OF
5 RATIONS

Operation Cobra

Above: A temporary field dressing station gives first aid to wounded of the advancing Allied forces.

Opposite: The town of St-Lô in Normandy in August 1944 with not an intact building in sight. The Operation Cobra breakout had St-Lô as its first important capture - of necessity as it was positioned on a strategic crossroads. Prior to engaging the determined defenders, the main lines of defence were carpet bombed then pounded by Allied artillery. American money paid for a new hospital after the war in some recompense for the devastation. At one point it was mooted that the town should remain a ruined monument to the invasion but it was rebuilt and its historic buildings restored.

On to Brittany

Above: The ruins of the town of Villers-Bocage are strewn around an important crossroads southeast of Caen. The road, recently cleared of rubble, is checked for mines.

Opposite: The main road through Avranches took high volumes of traffic en route to the new battlefront in Brittany.

Falaise

Above: Burnt-out Luftwaffe fighters lie in pieces in their maintenance hangar at Paris's Le Bourget Airport - at first a target for the attacking Allies who had set about destroying every airfield available to the Germans in France, and now for the Germans who wanted to deprive the Allies of a strategic base next to Paris.

Opposite: The town of Falaise, the centre of two weeks of fierce fighting, is a collection of ghostly ruins, pictured here after it was finally taken by Canadian forces on 17 August.

Paris liberated

Above: Senior Nazi officers are escorted by Free French Resistance under the watchful eyes of US troops. They provide a public spectacle outside the Hotel de Ville - the Town Hall of Paris.

Opposite: The liberation of Paris was completed on 25 August after 10 days of civil and military disobedience on all sides. The Allies had no plan to liberate Paris at this stage in the war, but wanted to make all haste to Berlin to end the conflict. The large population of Paris and intelligence reports that the German occupiers were poised to destroy the city around them, increased Allied determination to skirt round a potential Stalingrad. But a general strike in Paris from 15 August and overt action in the streets by the Free French Resistance, led the French commander, General Leclerc to disobey his battle orders from General Bradley and send an advance guard into the city with the promise of reinforcements to follow. Seeing that the die was cast, Bradley permitted Leclerc to fulfil his promise and in the event the German commander General Dietrich Von Choltitz disobeyed Hitler's orders to devastate the city; instead Choltitz surrendered.

Pockets of resistance

Above: Fighting in Paris was sporadic - the Germans had good military strength but used it sparingly; however they continued atrocities against the population to the very last and took refuge in pre-planned fortifications. The Free French hunted them down - the men here are advancing on a government building in which around 500 German soldiers had holed up and eventually surrendered.

Opposite: General de Gaulle flew in from his Algiers HQ to join the advance of French troops into Paris. He made a famous speech from the Hotel de Ville, emphasising the French role in liberating Paris. The following day, de Gaulle led a victory parade under the threat of sniper fire and took the salute with other Allied leaders in the Place de la Concorde.

Euphoria in Paris

Above: Cheering Parisians line the Champs Elysees and applaud the thousands of Allied troops parading to celebrate the liberation of the city: a sight to feed the propaganda machine and send a message to the German High Command.

Opposite: US tanks and transport line the square outside the Hotel de Ville, providing grandstand views for the elated people of Paris who are in a party mood.

German prisoner vilified

Above: Crowds jeer at this defeated German soldier marched at gunpoint through the northern town of St Mihiel, some distance east of Paris. The town would stir memories in the advancing Americans with its US Memorial Cemetery, containing the graves of over 400 American soldiers who died nearby in WWI.

Opposite: British tanks speed along the cobbled highway into Belgium while German prisoners are held at the roadside. Liberating Belgium was another piece of the jigsaw which would open a route to the River Rhine whilst giving the Allies the strategic port of Antwerp; however, although Belgium was liberated in the first week of September, Antwerp would not be effective as a port until the end of November, when the Scheldt Estuary area was finally cleared of doggedly resistant German troops.

Saipan falls

Above: On 15 September, US and Australian troops landed on the island of Morotai virtually unopposed; the beaches they chose were unsuited to unloading vehicles and equipment and the troops, including General Douglas MacArthur, had to wade chest-high through the sea. Morotai and its airfield were important to the later invasion of the Philippines and the Japanese knew this well: reinforcements poured into the island and although Allied forces controlled it, Japanese resistance continued until the end of the war, when around 600 remaining troops surrendered.

Opposite: An American tank patrols Garapan, Saipan's main city. Captured from the Japanese on 9 July 1944 after 24 days of bloody fighting, Saipan was one of the larger Mariana islands with a substantial civilian population, of which an estimated 22,000 Japanese died. The Japanese garrison numbered 30,000 and was wiped out in the battle which cost nearly 3,000 American lives with 10,000 wounded.

Peleliu landings

Above: On 17 September, US marines haul an anti-tank gun ashore from their landing craft in the invasion of Angaur, another of the Palau islands which had to be taken en route to the Philippines. The small garrison of Japanese fought hard but the battle was over by 30 September.

Opposite: The Battle of Peleliu, one of the small coral islands of Palau, was controversial; the airfield there was of little strategic importance and although the US attackers expected a quick victory, the Japanese had prepared for invasion with great care. From the first landing on 15 September, US forces faced determined opposition until 27 November when almost the entire Japanese garrison of 11,000 had been wiped out. This battle was a preview that prepared the US military for similar defensive tactics in Iwo Jima and Okinawa.

Rouen

Above: As British forces pushed north towards the Rhine they met many waterways that had to be bridged: engineers raised pontoon crossings to replace those demolished by retreating Germans. Here M10 tank destroyers of 77th Anti-Tank Regiment, 11th Armoured Division, cross a Bailey bridge over the Meuse-Escaut (Maas-Schelde) canal at Lille St Hubert (St Huibrechts) on 20 September 1944.

Opposite: The gothic spire of Rouen's historic cathedral points to the sky over the ruined city centre, which was severely damaged by Allied bombing on D-Day and its cathedral nearly destroyed.

Operation Market Garden

Above: Descending paratroops fill the skies jumping from C-47 transports with their equipment. Although brilliantly conceived, Market Garden differed from previous Allied campaigns with no rehearsals, no diversionary attacks and limited tactical planning that depended on achieving a sequence of separate objectives culminating in the bridge over the Rhine at Arnhem. Weaknesses quickly became apparent: commanders had ignored intelligence of German strength in the area, radio communications failed and deadlines lagged. Men fought with outstanding bravery and determination but at the end of the nine-day battle on 25 September there were nearly 8,000 casualties, dead, wounded or taken prisoner.

Opposite: Montgomery's daring plan to rush mechanised forces forward to the Rhine in the Netherlands centred on Operation Market Garden, the largest airborne attack in history, involving over 30,000 troops to secure the lower Rhine giving a direct route into Germany. US airborne troops are pictured in their transport plane before takeoff.

Destruction at Sea

Above: A dramatic photograph, taken on 24 August but not released to public view until mid-September, shows the last moments of two of the few remaining ships of the German Kriegsmarine in Western Europe: the heavy destroyer Z24 in company with the torpedo boat T24 had escaped destruction in the recent Battle of Ushant and both were discovered near the mouth of the River Gironde by Beaufighters of Coastal Command's RAF 236 and RCAF's 404 squadrons on a routine patrol out of Davidstow Moor. They attacked with rockets and cannon blazing in a hail of anti-aircraft fire from the enemy ships. All the Beaufighters were damaged but made it back to base. Later reconnaissance could only find oil-slicks remaining of the two German craft.

Opposite: Canadian troops row themselves ashore from this troopship in September. More than a million Canadians fought in the Allied forces across every theatre of war. Landing with the British on Juno, Gold and Sword on D-Day, they deployed northwards after the Battle of Falaise Gap, moving along the Channel coast reaching Dieppe, the scene of a military debacle that cost Canadians dearly in 1942, liberating Calais and ending in the Scheldt area where Canadians took a prominent part in ousting Nazi forces from September to October.

Festung Brest

Above: A captured German soldier hands over a 'safe conduct' dropped on the city to encourage surrender. Many others chose to fight until the end; the defenders were hardened paratroops commanded by a veteran of the Afrika Korps; in all, around 40,000 were estimated to be garrisoned in the port. Pulverised by artillery and aerial bombardment and flushed out in house-to-house fighting, the Germans surrendered on 19 September 1944.

Opposite: As Patton's Third US Army sped through Brittany, German occupation forces became trapped in the peninsula, taking refuge in the fortified coastal ports. Brest was a heavily fortified base for Germany's U-boats which harassed Allied shipping in the North Atlantic: here are pictured the massive concrete installations protecting Brest's submarine pens. Patton assigned his US VIII Corps to deal with the trapped Germans, and after capturing St Malo they arrived at Brest on 7 August.

U-Boat kill

Above: 500-ton U-boat 243 is surrounded by a hail of bullets as a depth-charge erupts in a plume close to the stricken vessel in the Bay of Biscay. This was the first kill of Flying Officer W B Tilley of the RAAF; along with his colleagues of 10 Squadron, he was trained to fly the Short Sunderland flying boat that, equipped with radar, could detect enemy submarines on the surface. The Sunderland carried out convoy escort duties throughout the war.

Opposite: A further wave of paratroopers creates a giant snowstorm over the Netherlands on 19 September, halfway through the doomed Operation Market Garden.

Dutch collaborators

As the Netherlands came under Allied control, Nazi collaborators were quickly arrested. Confusion over Dutch loyalty to the Allied cause was one of the key factors of Market Garden's failures. British intelligence believed the Dutch Resistance to be compromised by Nazi double agents and thus ignored critical information about German strength. Germany appointed an Austrian governor to rule the Netherlands and all political parties were banned except the National Socialist Party whose members were then promoted to key positions.

Opposite: A US 'Long Tom' 155mm field gun is towed across a Bailey bridge over the River Sieve outside Borgo San Lorenzo a short distance north of Florence in northern Italy. By 11 September, elements of the British 8th Army were advancing on the central section of the German Gothic Line - a fearsome defence around 10 miles deep that took advantage of the Apennines which cross Italy almost unbroken from east to west at this point. Despite a fierce two-pronged attack by the 8th and 5th Armies, the Gothic Line held, aided by terrible winter weather.

Slow progress in Holland

Above: Belgian police escort Nazi collaborators accompanied by crowds of civilians. The Allies liberated Brussels on 2 September and began their move east towards Germany. The Belgian people rounded up Nazi sympathisers in their wake.

Opposite: British infantry advance on the village of St Michielsgestel on the River Dommel, tributary to the Maas, a short distance south of 's-Hertogenbosch. In the aftermath of Market Garden the Allies slowly made progress in Holland.

Bruges liberated

Above: Canadian troops liberate Bruges in mid September and are cheered by the local people. The ancient city was of less importance than its connected port of Zeebrugge, which the German occupiers had made into a heavily defended fort - part of the Atlantic Wall; it was the beginning of November before

Zeebrugge fell. 15 days of fighting preceded the taking of Bruges but little damage was done to the town.

Opposite: In Grammont, a Belgian collaborator who worked for the Gestapo stands shamed in the city square.

Brussels falls

Above: Retreating from the Allied advance into Brussels at the beginning of September, the fleeing Germans set the Palais de Justice ablaze. But with the Allies' capture of Antwerp soon after, it was clear to all that the battle for the Lowlands was gathering momentum.

Opposite: An Allied tank crawls through the streets of newly-liberated Brussels carrying many high-spirited civilian passengers. Messages of support have been chalked onto the side of the tank.

Antwerp POWs

Above: Salvaged parts of V1 bombs that fell on southern England in great numbers from June 1944. These fragments were studied by M.A.P Experimental Station to discover possible deterrents. Despite the use of artillery barrages around the coast and patrols by specialist Tempest aircraft, nearly 1,000 'buzz-bombs' reached their targets causing 6,000 deaths and nearly 18,000 wounded. Capturing or destroying the launch sites in northern France and then in Holland helped out Britain, but retreating Germans used the flying bombs to devastate cities like Antwerp after its liberation.

Opposite: German prisoners march under guard through Antwerp. The speed of the Allied advance took the German defenders of Antwerp by surprise and the port was liberated on 4 September. Despite its importance to the Allied supply chain - by now seriously overstretched - it would take another three months to oust Germans from control of the waterway leading to the port, which was many miles upstream on the River Scheldt.

Calais surrenders

Above: A column of German prisoners marches through Aachen. With the failure of Montgomery's push to Berlin via Holland the initiative fell on US 1st Army, already at the French/German border; it was instructed to advance on the German industrial region, the Ruhr Valley. Substantial obstacles lay in the way, the largest being the Siegfried Line, a heavily fortified defence system built by Hitler in the 1930s opposite and north of the Maginot Line. The town of Aachen was incorporated into the Siegfried Line and was surrounded by concrete bunkers and gun emplacements. US forces attacked on 2 October,

intending to encircle the city but in fierce fighting that followed, the 5,000 German garrison had to be overcome building by building until the city finally surrendered on 21 October.

Opposite: Three Canadian soldiers march down the deserted Boulevard Pasteur in newly captured Calais, its famous clocktower in the background. The town was liberated on 1 October after the German garrison surrendered, having released 20,000 civilians during a 24-hour truce.

Aachen captured

Above: Civilian refugees presented further logistical problems for the Allied forces who encouraged the evacuation of cities like Aachen, relocating residents to temporary camps to avoid the inevitable disease spread with the loss of sanitation. However the refugees had to be carefully vetted for disguised German soldiers who might be escaping or have plans for sabotage.

Opposite: The quality of German forces defending Aachen was mixed - from hardened Panzer companies to units comprising young recruits and convalescents. However the fortifications of the city made up for the uneven quality of the troops and as well as slowing the US advance they cost around 5,000 Allied casualties. There was a strong will to defend the town - they were now on home ground rather than an alien occupying force; moreover Aachen was the seat of Charlemagne, founder of the First Reich, heavily symbolic to the Nazi regime.

Shell burst

Above: Advancing over open ground, this lucky infantryman survived the shell that burst right next to him.

Opposite: Squadron Leader JH Iremonger with members of 486 Squadron briefing his New Zealander pilots at their base, Grimbergen, in Belgium. This was one of five Tempest

Squadrons now located in Europe which had made its name defending Britain against V1 flying bombs. The Hawker Tempest, designed by Sidney Camm and based on the Typhoon, was fast at low altitude - and thus able to keep pace with the rocket-propelled V1s; the Tempest pilots learned the weak points of the buzz-bombs and had excellent kill-rates.

Manila Bay

Above: Carrier aircraft of Admiral William F Halsey's third Pacific Fleet swept the island of Luzon in the heart of the Philippines on 20 September and are seen here striking in great force at shipping in Manila Bay; later they continued the attack in Subic Bay and at enemy installations at Clark Field and Nichols Field near Manila, and at the Cavite Naval Base. Taking the enemy by surprise, this attack caused severe losses to the Japanese, with over 200 aircraft destroyed, 11 ships sunk and nearly 30 more damaged - all with the loss of just 15 US aircraft.

Opposite: In 1944, 62-year-old Franklin Delano Roosevelt stood for an unprecedented fourth term and was re-elected President, despite his declining health. Excited service personnel track the progress of the election in the US forces social club - hosted at Rainbow Corner on Shaftesbury Avenue in London's Soho. There they had access to food, dancing and attractive companions 24 hours a day.

Front line in Brabant

Above: Despite the steady
withdrawal of German
forces from the lowlands of
Holland and Belgium, they
continued to wreak damage
with the terrifying V1 and V2
rockets which were launched
many miles from the front.
Here civilian casualties
killed in a Belgian town
are recovered by shocked
compatriots.

Opposite: Polish infantry
engage German forces with
Bren gun and machine gun
under the cover of a wrecked
Brabant farmhouse near
Hooge Zwaluwe in Holland,
no more than 400 yards
from the German front line.

Gelsenkirchen refinery in ruins

Above: German troops surrender to US forces as the advance into Germany continues. It wasn't always this easy: the series of fierce battles fought between US and German forces in the Hürtgen Forest, which became the longest battle on German ground during World War II and the longest single battle the US Army has ever fought in its history, lasted for five months during an intensely cold winter.

Opposite: The oil refinery at Gelsenkirchen was continuously attacked during the autumn of 1944. While the state of the installation in the photograph is not easy to determine, the number of bomb craters clearly visible shows the intensity of the bombardment intended to deprive Germany of vital fuel supplies.

Flying Fortress in action

Above: In late autumn the pressure of Allied bombing over German industrial areas was overwhelming: on this occasion more than 1000 B-17 and B-24s attacked vital railway marshalling yards near Osnabriick in Germany. Allied air forces now demonstrated total air supremacy in both bomber and fighter forces.

Opposite: A B-17 Flying Fortress is photographed just after dropping its bombs on the Bettenhausen ordnance plant near Kassel in Germany on 2 October. The target zone is outlined and smoke plumes from the burning installation.

Warsaw uprising collapses

Above: In August 1944, the Polish resistance movement launched their second uprising against the Nazi occupiers in Warsaw, intending to make their contribution to the advancing Russian liberators. The Russians arrived on the other side of the Vistula in September and made no move to liberate the city. The Polish resistance had no choice but to capitulate in October and when the Russians entered the city they found 85% of it in ruins. Around 200,000 citizens died in the uprising. Looking on from the West, it was suspected that

Stalin deliberately watched the Polish position weaken in order to redefine Russian borders - something he had on his agenda since meeting with Churchill and Roosevelt at the Tehran Conference at the end of 1943.

Opposite: British troops dig-in near the River Maas in Holland at the end of November. The lowlands, interlined with canals and rivers, often flooded for defence by the Germans, made the advance difficult during the winter.

Rhine crossing destroyed

Above: A 9th Air Force B-26 Marauder pictured on 19 November where it has just successfully bombed the Neuenberg rail crossing over the Rhine at the German border east of the Belfort Gap. The US 7th Army was advancing towards this point en route to Germany. The 9th Air Force was based in France and was the main Allied tactical force, supporting troops from D-Day onwards.

Opposite: British armour rumbles past a US post on its way to the front line.

Target of opportunity

Above: To the right of this picture can be seen the railway marshalling yards of Friedberg, north of Frankfurt am Main. During December, few planned missions were flown against them but the yards were a regular 'target of opportunity'. Here 500-pound bombs dropped from a B-17 Flying Fortress head for their destination thousands of feet below.

Opposite: Bomber crews had their good days and many bad ones, casualties were high and flying conditions always uncomfortable and hazardous for the crew. The end could come suddenly as with this B-24 Liberator, which is breaking up in the air after being hit by flak over Germany. Fuel tanks were spread through the fuselage giving a tendency for the craft to catch fire or explode. The typical 10-man crew had little chance of survival.

St Nazaire evacuation

French and American Officers discuss the truce, agreed to allow civilians to be transported from the encircled bastion of St Nazaire on the Atlantic coast, with Hauptmann D Mueller who represented the town's Nazi commander; it was agreed that trains could come and go from the town twice a day for 5 days while an hour's ceasefire was observed. St Nazaire was a strategic base for Germany's Kriegsmarine and its submarine fleet. The port was severely disabled in a commando raid in 1943 but the garrison held out from September 1944 until several days after the armistice in 1945.

A German officer surrenders his position at Metz to US 3rd Army forces in November 1944. The city, capital of the Lorraine region of France was annexed to the Reich early in the war and heavily fortified. Metz occupied a strategic position at the confluence of the Moselle and Seille rivers with roads and railways also converging. Allied forces arrived at the city in September but took many weeks to completely capture all its fortifications.

V1 aftermath

Above: On Christmas Eve 1944, specially modified Luftwaffe Heinkel H-111s carrying 45 V1 rockets launched them off the Lincolnshire coast. Half an hour later 31 buzz-bombs found targets in the north of England, 15 of them on Greater Manchester. The havoc created by these bombs can be seen here; a total of 27 people died and 49 were seriously injured during this raid.

Opposite: The last of the German forts, 'Jeanne d'Arc', defending Metz finally capitulated on 13 December. Besieging the forts had not cost the Allies too dearly but the defence of Metz slowed up the advance on Germany and gave the Wehrmacht time to gather itself for a major counterattack. US infantry finally take control of the entire city.

Battle of the Bulge

Right: On 16 December the German army launched a counter-offensive that took Allied Command completely by surprise. Advances by the Allies on all fronts compressed the German armies on home ground, consolidating and concentrating their strength. Hitler came up with a plan to punch through the Ardennes to retake Antwerp, cut off the supply chain to the Allied armies and force them into a truce in the bitter winter conditions. The success of this 'Operation Rhine Watch' was totally dependent on speed and surprise. At the outset, German armoured infantry achieved some success with the intricately planned attack. As predicted, the poor weather deprived the Allies of vital air cover and the diversionary tactics deployed by the Germans concealed their true intent, aided by the absence of information from local resistance fighters or Ultra traffic. Furthermore the Allied forces occupying the Ardennes region were thinly spread novice troops or recuperating veterans.

Opposite: In the centre of the attack zone was the Belgian town of Bastogne, located on a strategic crossroads which the attacking Germans made an essential objective. Despite the element of surprise and the mixed quality of the US troops, their resistance to the surprise attack was determined and the fighting, during what became known as The Battle of the Bulge, was intense. American forces held onto Bastogne even after the town was enveloped by the German advance. Occupants of the town fled towards Allied lines.

Improved artillery

Above: GIs huddle in their coats riding the truck towing an anti-tank gun into this Belgian town shrouded in snow. The intense cold of the winter during the weeks of the Battle of the Bulge meant troops had to carefully maintain their weaponry and attend to their vehicles, running the engines regularly to avoid the sump-oil and fuel lines freezing.

Opposite: An anti-aircraft artillery piece is brought to bear in close fighting during the Battle of the Bulge. The recent revolutionary new armament, the proximity fuse was first used by field artillery in the Battle. After the fuses' startling success in anti-aircraft ordnance against V1 bombs, the Pentagon was desperate to avoid the mechanism falling into enemy hands and therefore resistant to its deployment in artillery; but Eisenhower insisted and the new technology vastly improved the efficiency of Allied bombardments because the shells exploded before they hit the ground but near to substantial military targets.

Freezing in the Ardennes

Above: The frozen corpse of a German soldier appears still to be in a firing position. The conditions of fighting during the Battle of the Bulge were dreadful and although both sides showed great determination, morale was hard to maintain. In the first day of fighting, German troops overran and captured around 9,000 US troops, while German advance guard dressed in US uniforms set about causing confusion and chaos. On the German side, planned tactical operations went astray when a parachute force was widely spread around a missed drop zone; ironically this gave the Allies an impression of a much larger attack.

Opposite: The 101st Airborne were one of the tenacious units holding Bastogne and fought off these unfortunate attackers whose bodies lie frozen in the snow. The Americans were in dire circumstances, down to 10 rounds of ammunition per gun per day, but fortunately the weather improved, allowing supplies to be dropped by parachute, relieving shortages of food, ammunition and medical supplies. A team of medics flew in by glider to attend to the many wounded. Eventually, elements of Patton's Third Army broke through to relieve Bastogne on 26 December.

Anhalter Bahnhof Berlin

Above: As the Allies ground away on the Western Front, the Russians were steadily moving towards Berlin in the east. Eisenhower decided to increase the pressure on the capital by a devastating bombing campaign early in 1945. Almost 1,000 B-17 bombers of the Eighth Air Force, protected by P-51 Mustangs attacked the Berlin railway system on 3 February, having been informed that the German Sixth Panzer Army was moving through Berlin by train on its way to the Eastern Front. The raid killed between 2,500 and 3,000 people and made 120,000 homeless. Anhalter Station, pictured here, was destroyed.

Opposite: Troops of General Patton's Third Army trudge through the winter snow in January 1945 on their way to rendezvous with Montgomery's 21st Army Group at Houffalize, Belgium, effectively closing down the German offensive - which, having suffered serious losses, was running out of steam. Hitler finally allowed his battle-weary troops to retreat on 7 January and on 25 January the Battle of the Bulge was finally over - the most costly American military engagement to date in the war. But for Germany it was the final turning point, this gamble exhausted its military reserves and put the Luftwaffe beyond recovery.

Battle of Iwo Jima

Opposite: Seaborne US invasion forces head for the beaches of Iwo Jima on the morning of 19 February. The assault on Iwo Jima was a turning point in the Pacific war as Japanese sovereign territory was being invaded for the first time in the war. After capturing the Marianas in 1944, the US was ready to focus on Japan itself. Iwo Jima's three airfields made it a potent attack base for Japanese aircraft and would make it a perfect strategic airbase for assault on Japan. Over 70 days of aerial bombardment preceded the invasion and heavy naval guns pounded the Japanese positions for three days before. In the first wave, 30,000 US troops landed in the first day.

Above: Realising the strategic importance of the island to the advancing Allies, the Japanese increased the garrison to 18,000 and a defensive plan was initiated. The Japanese commander designed his fortifications to take advantage of the island's topography, especially the extinct volcano Mt Suribachi, where a network of tunnels and gun emplacements enabled the defenders to survive the pulverising American bombardment and to mount a strong defence against infantry attack.

Iconic moment on Iwo Jima

Opposite: Five days after the invasion, US forces on Iwo Jima numbered 70,000 and on 23 February a platoon of marines scaled Mt Suribachi and raised the Stars and Stripes at its summit. This moment was captured by photographer Louis R Lowery and achieved iconic status for the American people in general and US forces in particular. The battle would last another month; the last assault by the Japanese being on 25 March. Bitter fighting on both sides resulted in many casualties: of the total Japanese military of around 22,000 only a couple of hundred were captured alive - it is assumed the rest died. Of the final number of US troops engaged (110,000), 26,000 became casualties, 7,000 of them fatalities.

Above: The capture of the Marianas Islands in 1944 enabled Admiral Nimitz to set up his HQ on Guam with harbour facilities for a third of the US Pacific Fleet. This was followed by the building of Isely Field on Saipan - the first of five airbases in the Marianas which would accommodate the B-29 Superfortresses whose bombs ended the Japanese military regime. Here, more material and machinery are unloaded through the bow doors of LSTs directly onto the quay.

Battle of Okinawa

Above: This photograph show the horrific task the US troops faced on Okinawa, often taking out the Japanese positions one at a time, using explosives and facing suicidal counterattacks that might come without warning. Americans landed on the Island on 1 April and secured it on 21 June. In addition to the loss of over 100,000 troops, the Japanese suffered horrific civilian casualties which have never been defined but were estimated between 40-150,000.

Opposite: The closing chapter of the war with Japan was preceded by the Battle of Okinawa: having rolled up the Pacific islands occupied by Japan and its dependency Iwo Jima, US forces now struck at the homeland, seeking a base on the Ryukyu Islands - the archipelago that stretches south from the main island group. Okinawa, the best suited for such a base was heavily garrisoned and fiercely defended. It was the determined and often suicidal fighting of the Japanese on Okinawa that convinced the Allies that the loss of life caused by use of atomic weapons would balance out a long-drawn-out final battle that Japan could not win but in which it would never concede defeat.

Intense fighting in Manila

Some of the most intense and ferocious fighting of the Pacific conflict took place as US and Filipino forces battled with the Japanese in the streets of Manila. Battle commenced on 3 February and, after much bloodshed, ended on 3 March. The street fighting was reminiscent of Stalingrad and over 100,000 civilians died, either as collateral damage or resulting from deliberate Japanese action. Much of Manila's unique ancient heritage was destroyed as the Japanese defenders used the Intramuros as their bastion. In these pictures, a wounded GI is carried by stretcher to a dressing station in City Hall, while opposite, a blown up bridge droops into the river and plumes of smoke rise from the devastated city.

Advancing from Belgium

Above: British and Dutch infantry man a defensive perimeter around this bridge in Belgium as a Sherman M4 tank surges forward into attack.

Opposite: Snowfall on this Belgian airfield didn't halt RAF bomber operations as the attrition of German production and communications continued through the spring of 1945.

Nearing the German border

Above: Amphibious 'Buffaloes' deliver supplies to Canadian troops in the flooded estuary of the Scheldt. This tracked vehicle first saw service in the Pacific when it was used as a supply vehicle; but the ability of its tracks to emerge from water and run on a soft surface led to more widespread use as a troop carrier.

Opposite: A motorised anti-tank gun of the British Second Army on station in the Dutch town of Susteren in the south-eastern province of Limburg. A transport convoy heads towards Germany.

Red Army offensive speeds up

Above: Not everyone was as happy to see the Red Army liberators as these citizens of Rostov when the city was recaptured from the Nazis in 1943. The end of the German terrorizing of the Slavic Untermenschen was some cause for celebration, although the advancing Soviet troops brought their own terror to the civilian populations.

Opposite: In January the Red Army broke out from captured Warsaw and began a series of offensives that would culminate in the capture of Berlin in April. In the so-called Oder-Vistula offensive, the Soviets outnumbered Germans 5-1. Not only did they have superiority in numbers, their vast quantity of armour enabled them to move with a speed equivalent to the German Blitzkrieg. However casualties were high - in the 23 days the Russians suffered 194,000 casualties and lost 1,267 tanks and assault guns.

Yalta Conference

Left: In February 1945, the historic meeting of Allied leaders took place in Yalta in the Black Sea area of the Russian Crimea. Winston Churchill, Franklin D Roosevelt and Josef Stalin decided the final fate of Germany: it was to be divided into four zones of influence supervised by each of the main Allied powers, including France. Despite the bonhomie, Churchill deeply distrusted Stalin; Roosevelt was more trusting and supportive of Stalin. Once again, Churchill's instincts were suppressed by the judgement of others. History proved him right once more.

Opposite: Stalin and Roosevelt discuss the post-war settlement in Europe at the Yalta Conference in February 1945.

Berlin pounded from the air

Above: Flying Fortresses in formation over Germany. Every day that weather conditions permitted, as many as 1,500 bombers and fighter escorts would fly bombing missions over Germany, directed at specific targets but often finding 'targets of opportunity' if unable to identify their designated location.

Opposite: Bombs dropped by this USAAF B-17 erupt as they land on Berlin, casting a huge pall of smoke and dust over the city. The German capital became a focus for bombing as Allied troops drew nearer; it was feared that the city would be fiercely defended so Allied High Command was determined to crush all opposition.

Operation Plunder

Above: On 23 March 1945 General Montgomery set in motion Operation Plunder, the much-awaited crossing of the Rhine into Germany's heartland. In the preceding weeks the landing area designated for the bridgehead had been bombarded, virtually destroying the towns of Wesel and Rees. Here Gordon Highlanders, elements of 21st Army Group, patrol through the ruins of Rees which was secured by fierce house-to-house fighting.

Opposite: The carefully planned offensive was successful and within four days the Allied bridgehead was 35 miles (55 km) wide and 20 miles (30 km) deep.

Banks of the Rhine

Above: British troops file over the levee to their embarkation point on the west bank of the Rhine.

Opposite: Field artillery units stand by their guns ready to give support to the next phase of Operation Plunder.

YOU ARE NOW
CROSSING THE
RHINE RIVER
THROUGH COURTESY
OF 'E' CO. 17 ARMD
ENGR. BN. AND
'C' CO. 202
ENGR. C. BN.

Temporary crossing

Above: US engineers had this pontoon bridge over the Rhine operational during the first day of the crossing. The 972-feet-long bridge was created in record time and was one of three that the Allied forces deployed early in Operation Plunder.

Opposite: With the Allied forces crossing the Rhine in overwhelming numbers and using the bridges to move heavy armour into place, German opposition varied but there was much fierce fighting and deadly machine gun defence. Here infantry of the US 7th Army provide covering fire from the west bank of the Rhine as their fellow soldiers cross.

Allies pour into Germany

Above: Eisenhower's 'Broad Front' assault and attack over the Rhine enabled overwhelming land forces to break into Germany from the west - a crushing blow to German morale and local commanders quickly realised their position was untenable.

Opposite: Churchill visited the front line on numerous occasions to make a personal appraisal of the tactical situation and to encourage his forces. On 25 March he arrived at Montgomery's HQ and, with him and a number of US officers, crossed the Rhine by boat to an area still controlled by German forces; targeted by artillery they swiftly withdrew.

Thousands captured

Above: German soldiers making a determined defence nevertheless knew that their cause was lost; furthermore they knew that if there was a choice between being captured by Americans or Russians, they would sooner give themselves up to US or British forces. Thousands of German prisoners were taken as the Allies advanced.

Opposite: Amid the ruins of Wesel, British commandos operate machine guns while waiting to be relieved by reinforcements after they spearheaded the crossing of the Rhine in assault boats on the night of 23 March.

Crushed survivors

Above: Hitler tried to rally his troops on 30 March with a message encouraging 'fanatic determination' to defend Berlin and achieve victory. Whether anybody believed his words, many Germans fought on - especially on the Eastern Front where the Russian advance was ruthless. Here, Patton's forces escort German prisoners to holding camps.

Opposite: Around 20,000 German prisoners of war wait for marching orders in the grounds of a German military academy near the Rhine.

Operation Varsity

Above: Soon after the main assault began on the Rhine, US and British airborne troops parachuted into forward positions to disrupt German defence and occupy strategic positions. After the Market Garden fiasco Montgomery could not afford another failure at this critical point in the war. Operation Varsity on 24 March was the biggest single airborne operation of all time when 16,000 troops jumped into German territory.

Here, a small fraction of the several thousand transport planes pass overhead watched by awestruck civilians. The fleet of aircraft stretched for 500 miles.

Opposite: British infantry advance into Germany on foot after crossing the Rhine.

Flag of surrender

Above: The steamroller advance of the Allies in the west was matched in the east by Russian forces overwhelming the exhausted and by now poorly equipped German troops fighting for their survival and every metre of their territory. By mid-April, General Zukhov's armies in the north had reached the Oder while the Red Army in the south now held Vienna. On 15 April, the heaviest artillery barrage in history marked the start of the final Russian advance on Berlin and 10 days later the capital would be encircled by the Allied forces which linked up at Torgau on the River Elbe.

Opposite: Citizens of the Rhine Province town of Rheydt meet Allied troops with white flags. Known to be the birthplace of Joseph Goebbels and the founder of Junkers, the town's civilians were uncertain of how they would be treated.

Churchill visits Jülich

Above: The fortifications of Jülich led to its being bombed to oblivion by the advancing Allies who assumed that the town, located strategically on the River Rur, a tributary to the Meuse, would be a major obstacle to their advance. Churchill visited the town after it had been captured in February and Eisenhower was also photographed among the ruins.

Opposite: By 4 March, US troops had entered the strategically important city of Trier. After being stalled by the battle for Metz and the Battle of the Bulge, the next step was to secure and advance from the Saar-Moselle triangle. Trier was the

prize that followed this successful action. It is reported that Eisenhower, while unaware that Patton's forces had taken the city, instructed him to bypass the city, fearing its capture would require four divisions and could result in another delay like Metz. Patton's reply was, 'Have taken Trier with two divisions. What do you want me to do? Give it back?' The surrendering Germans had some reason to be nervous; they could recall the poor treatment given to Allied prisoners who had marched from Dunkirk to Trier to be despatched to labour and prison camps around Germany.

Volkssturm

Left: This 14-year-old German boy soldier was captured in the March assault on the Siegfried Line. With Wehrmacht military reserves exhausted, the Volkssturm militia provided combat troops from their ranks of juveniles and retirees.

Opposite: British and Canadian troops spread southeastwards from the lowlands of Holland and Belgium, reaching Udem east of the Rhine on 27 February then moving on to capture Kervenheim. Here British infantry brew up outside Udem while a rifleman keeps lookout.

Weapons amnesty

Opposite: The Allies controlled a significant area of Germany by April 1945 and had to establish a workable government under military jurisdiction. Pictured here, a German policeman accepts weapons handed in by civilians under American supervision in the town of Bad Godesberg which was the first major town to surrender to the Allies without armed resistance. It was also the location of a historic meeting between Chamberlain and Hitler in 1938 when they met to discuss the Sudetenland crisis.

Above: Citizens of Saarbrucken congregate with their few possessions in the centre of the destroyed city. Most of its population of 135,000 fled in the face of the Allied aerial onslaught and ground attack in March 1945.

Landing zone

Above: Parachutes litter the landing zone east of the Rhine during Operation Varsity.

Opposite: A cocktail mixture of high explosive and incendiary bombs descends on Gladbeck in the industrial Ruhr region of Germany. Gladbeck's railway marshalling yards were vital to the distribution of coal from the town's mines. 1,250 B-17s and B-24s of the Eighth USAAF carried out the raid on 23 March escorted by 350 P-51 Mustang fighter aircraft.

Guarding prisoners

Above: Densely packed German prisoners of war are guarded vigilantly under the sights of this US soldier's machine gun.

Opposite: Canadian troops drive their tracked personnel carrier through newly captured Emmerich in early April 1945. The town, on the north bank of the Rhine, was the last main settlement on the river before flowing into Holland. Fiercely defended by German paratroops, the town eventually gave way to superior Allied strength.

POWs released

Above: Altengrabow Camp, Stalag XIA, housed 20,000 Allied prisoners including 2,000 British and Americans. It was first used in WWI and the conditions were poor and overcrowded; just before liberation there was an outbreak of typhus. By this point in the war, Germany was very short of food and the prisoners were starving.

Opposite: British POWs in April 1945 after being liberated from Stalag 11B near Fallingbostel; all the prisoners were suffering from malnutrition and had to be weaned carefully back to a normal diet. Red Cross parcels were sent to all POW camps and should have been distributed in accord with the Geneva Convention. In reality, most were diverted by the German authorities.

Russian prisoners set free

Above: Russian POWs pour out of the unlocked gates of their prison camp to greet their liberators in April 1945. This camp held 9,000 prisoners but the death toll had been terrible as starvation and typhus were rampant. Some accounts suggest that 30,000 Russians died in Stalags XIB and XID alone.

Opposite: The Allied campaign in Italy was now focused on crushing the northern industrial area which was still stoutly defended and aided by the terrain. Tactical bombing missions were flown daily by 12th Air Force while 15th Air Force's B-17s and B-24s flew strategic missions over northern Italy and southern Europe generally. The close formation flying of the strategic bombers gave the crews very uncomfortable experiences like this, pictured, where a Liberator is seen taking a direct hit from flak over northern Italy, losing a wing before plunging to earth.

Beast of Belsen

Above: The German military authorities understood how the Allies would view the death camps and some efforts were made to conceal them. In the last months of the war, concentration camps in the East of Germany and Poland were evacuated, their occupants forced to march deep into Germany under terrible conditions that killed many thousands. Here a mass grave is uncovered - the last resting place of prisoners on their way to Bergen-Belsen who died in transit. Buried by their surviving inmates, who were then shot and added to the burial.

Opposite: Allied troops advancing through Germany began their discovery of the gruesome Nazi death camps; the POW camps were bad enough, but the dawning realisation of the scale of the Nazi extermination programme horrified the world. Josef Kramer, nicknamed the Beast of Belsen, was captured at Bergen-Belsen. He was tried for war crimes, convicted and hanged in December 1945.

Horror of death camps

Above: The liberation of the Nazi prison camps presented a huge challenge to the Allies; the prisoners were in terrible physical condition and continued to die in large numbers after being liberated. Of those that survived, most were vast distances from their home, which very probably had been destroyed, along with the relatives, neighbours or other possible support for these shattered people. Repatriating Allied POWs was relatively straightforward, but the civilians generally continued to live in camps, moving from the concentration camps into displaced persons centres, while the Red Cross and other organisations supported their search for lost relatives and a way to return home.

Opposite: Photographs like this helped people understand the scale and horror of the death camps: the personal possessions of the murdered inmates, such as these shoes, were stock-piled in storage in their tens of thousands.

Heligoland razed

Above: The airfield on the German island of Dune disappears under a cloud of smoke and debris caused by a concentrated bombardment of nearly 1,000 RAF bombers. Heligoland, a group of rocky islands, originally fortified by the British, acted as a strategic base for Germany in WWII, in particular protecting the approach to the Kiel Canal and German North Sea ports whilst giving a valuable striking base for targets in the North Sea and northern Britain. The islands were heavily garrisoned and equipped with artillery and anti-aircraft.

Submarines and motor torpedo boats were based there. After the raids on 18 and 19 April, the fortifications were virtually destroyed and the islands were uninhabitable for many years.

Opposite: In northern Germany, close to the River Elbe, mechanised troops of the 15th Scottish Division enveloped then cleared the town of Uelzen on 19 April. Uelzen hosted a concentration camp and was strategically placed on the Mittelland Canal.

Allies link up

Above: On 25 April, US and Soviet troops linked up at the town of Torgau on the River Elbe. This photograph, staged for the press had great symbolism for the Allied world: the handshake of infantry on the demolished bridge showed that a shattered Europe could be restored.

Opposite: Russian and US officers talk animatedly to Ann Stringer, Universal Press's front line correspondent. Ordered back to Paris on 25 April, she managed to requisition a military intelligence plane that flew her to Torgau where she tracked down the meeting point of the two armies. She then hitched a ride on a C-47 aircraft back to Paris, scooping the story for the world press. The return to Paris would have mixed feelings as her husband William, a Reuters correspondent, was killed there during the city's liberation.

Reichstag

Opposite: The link-up of the Allied armies sealed the doom on an overwhelmed Germany, everywhere in ruins. Like the Reichstag parliament building in Berlin pictured here, Hitler's glorious Third Reich was now an empty shell. On 30 April, Adolf Hitler and his bride of less than 48 hours, Eva Braun, committed suicide in the Führer's Berlin bunker. On 7 May in Reims, France, General Jodl signed Germany's surrender on behalf of Hitler's successor Admiral Karl Dönitz.

Above: The Dutch were already celebrating their liberation as of 5 May. A victory parade in Utrecht was fired on by Nazi sympathisers; Dutch freedom fighters interrogate a man found in the building from which the shots were fired.

Red Army victory parade

Above: Marshal Joseph Stalin ordered a victory parade in Red Square on 24 June - a massive military display that honoured Soviet Marshals Zhukov and Rokossovsky and culminated in captured Nazi banners being cast down in front of the Mausoleum.

Opposite: The announcement of VE Day brought thousands of Americans into New York City's Times Square to celebrate the unconditional surrender of Germany.

VE Day at last

Opposite: Spirits ran high in London with the announcement by Winston Churchill on 8 June that the war in Europe was at an end. Westminster and the West End of London filled with jubilant people; forming a human pyramid on a truck held no fear for those who survived the Blitz!

Above: Winston Churchill made his historic broadcast to the nation from the Cabinet Room, 10 Downing St on 8 May announcing Victory in Europe. The King gave a speech from Buckingham Palace to thousands assembled in the Mall and in Trafalgar Square. Churchill and members of his Cabinet then appeared on the balcony of the Ministry of Health to greet the crowds in Whitehall. Ever focused, Churchill addressed the task ahead - to subdue treacherous Japan.

The King speaks

Opposite: The crowds in Trafalgar Square stand silently listening to the words of King George VI that were being relayed from Buckingham Palace to a local Tannoy system. Ecstatic crowds cheered the Royal Family who waved from the Palace balcony.

Above: This British sergeant, recently released from a German POW camp, is greeted by his family and receives a hero's welcome in his Devon village. Spick and span in a new uniform and smiling broadly, no one could guess the ordeal men like him had been enduring during their incarceration.

Street party

While the entire civilian population of Britain celebrated VE day with formal events and neighbourhood street parties, the untold damage of the war needed attention at home and abroad; the work of Allied troops was not over in Europe: the armies of occupation supervised German prisoners, protected civilian populations and aided the restoration of the transport infrastructure and other essential services.

Above: Dressed in their best clothes and with the street decorated with bunting and a V for victory chalked on the cobbles, this Leeds street enjoys their victory celebration.

Opposite: Further south in the London suburb of Brockley, a group of children sit at their V-shaped table to enjoy their VE Day party.

Battle for New Guinea

Opposite: While conflict subsided in the European and Mediterranean theatres of war, the Allies remained engaged in fierce and deadly combat with Japan in the Far East. Australian troops were fighting in the jungle of New Guinea under the most difficult conditions resulting in many casualties.

Above: Australian forces begin their seaborne landings on the island of Tarakan, Borneo on 1 May 1945. The invasion was well-executed though there were problems in landing; the Allies had overwhelming numbers by comparison with the Japanese garrison because fierce resistance was expected. Tarakan's oilfields were strategically important and the Allies hoped to make good use of the island's airfield. This picture shows the effectiveness of the modified landing craft that were equipped with rockets; these LCMRs could deliver devastating barrages with lightning speed, just before attacking infantry landed. Pockets of Japanese soldiers held out until 21 June.

Rotterdam liberated

Above: Dutch civilians crowd onto this Canadian armoured vehicle as it rolls through Rotterdam; the tricolour flags of the Netherlands are displayed everywhere in contrast to four years of the hated swastika.

Opposite: Delighted citizens of Rotterdam flock to meet a Canadian road convoy loaded with food and supplies as it enters the newly liberated city. German forces in the Netherlands negotiated their surrender on 4 May to take effect the next day which has been celebrated as Liberation Day in the Netherlands ever since.

Denmark set free

Above: Allied forces landed in Denmark to take over the security of the country because of substantial Nazi occupation forces garrisoned there. Although no force had to be used by Allies against the Germans, the internal politics of Denmark led to continuing violence as Nazi supporters were rounded up by the Danish resistance and the so-called Hipos mounted spite attacks. The heavy cruiser *Prinz Eugen*, one of the few Kriegsmarine vessels to survive the war, was in the port of Copenhagen and was handed over to the US Navy later in the year: she became part of the nuclear test programme in the Pacific and after radioactive contamination was sunk.

Opposite: A German U-Boat 532 arrives in the Liverpool docks after surrendering in the Atlantic on 10 May. The long-distance submarine was one of 11 sent to the Indian Ocean in July 1943 in support of Japan. Of the 11 only 5 made it to the base in Batavia where they hunted Allied shipping. The U-Boat set out for Europe in January 1945 with a crew of over 40 and a 140-ton cargo of tungsten and bales of raw rubber. On 5 May, German submarines assigned to Asia received the code 'Lübeck' signifying that hostilities had ended.

Concrete Battleship

Above: Fort Drum, nicknamed the Concrete Battleship, was a defensive installation built on a tiny island in Manila Bay to cover its approaches and the US garrison of Corregidor. The heavily fortified installation bristled with guns and fought hard to resist the Japanese who took it in 1942. When Allied forces recaptured Corregidor in February 1945, Fort Drum remained in the control of the Japanese until 13 April when US forces approached, avoided its heavy guns and landed; a landing craft tanker was called into use and several thousand gallons of an inflammable mixture were poured into the ventilation system and TNT charges set, creating an explosive inferno that wrecked the fort and killed its garrison. In this remarkable photograph, taken by Acme War Pool Correspondent, Stanley Troutman, the LCM can be seen in the foreground while infantry cover the engineers who are feeding the fuel into the vents and setting their charges.

Opposite: At the end of April the Burma campaign was at a turning point with Allied forces advancing down the Irawaddy River towards the capital of Rangoon. Lord Louis Mountbatten, supreme commander in the region and his principal general, Sir William Slim, were anxious to capture Rangoon before the start of the monsoon when the weather would favour Japanese defenders. In the end, despite poor weather, their plan to liberate Rangoon worked and on 3 May the city was taken by Gurkha paratroops without resistance. Here British XXXIII Corps battle floods on the road to Prome, an important bridgehead on the Irawaddy.

New rule in Berlin

Above: Occupying Soviet forces in Berlin made it clear to the local citizenry that they were under a new regime - it was their turn to be occupied and by July 1945 it was public knowledge that Russia would rule nearly half of Germany and a substantial part of the capital. A giant portrait of Stalin is displayed in front of the the Adlon Hotel on Unter den Linden in the centre of the city: the hotel, one of the most famous in Europe, survived the battle for Berlin but fell victim to carousing Russian soldiers in May who set it ablaze leaving it a ruined shell.

Opposite: Signposts in Russian direct the occupying forces to the Reichstag and Unter den Linden from this junction next to the Kaiserin Augusta Gedächtniskirche on the Kurfürstendamm in Berlin's ruined centre.

Borneo

Opposite: Australian infantry march into a liberated plantation on Labuan Island, Borneo in June 1945. The Japanese garrison was under-strength but held out in a pocket in a swampy area of the island. Labuan's strategic position would return control of the Bay of Brunei to the Allies along with the area's oilfields and rubber plantations.

Above: The Allied Pacific Fleet was subject to ceaseless attacks by Japanese Kamikaze suicide missions. These could vary from bomb-carrying fighter aircraft to piloted rocket-propelled bombs. Here, following a Kamikaze attack on a British aircraft carrier of the Pacific Fleet the wreckage is being cleared away after a deck fire was extinguished. Around 4,000 Japanese died in Kamikaze missions. US carriers depended on their anti-aircraft guns and as much fighter cover as they could muster; unlike their British counterparts which had steel flightdecks, the US carriers had wooden decks which could be severely damaged in a Kamikaze attack. The last Kamikaze mission flew on 15 August.

Potsdam Conference

Left: The famous Potsdam Conference brought new US President Harry S Truman to Europe to meet with Winston Churchill and Joseph Stalin to settle the fate of Germany and its people. Just a few weeks after VE Day the shape of Allied leadership would be changed. The conference lasted from 17 July to 2 August; at the end of it, Churchill would no longer be British Prime Minister. Truman, like Churchill, held different views from Roosevelt and Stalin would no longer enjoy a placatory compliance from a very different US President. Truman enraged the Russian leader by withholding the details of the atomic bomb that America had successfully tested and which Truman and Churchill had agreed to deploy against Japan if the Potsdam Declaration failed to gain unconditional Japanese surrender.

Opposite: During the Potsdam Conference, Churchill visited the site of Hitler's bunker in Berlin, lowering himself gingerly in the chair pictured, said to be one of Hitler's. Much moved by the sights of the capital, he reflected that in different circumstances, 10 Downing Street could have met a similar fate.

Balikpapan landings

Above: Amphibious craft deliver elements of the Australian Seventh Division to the shore east of Balikpapan, a key oil port on the island of Borneo. The offensive, supported by US naval bombardment, began on 1 July and though heavily outnumbered, Japanese defeat was not completed until 21 July, making the Battle of Balikpapan one of the last major actions of the war.

Opposite: A Bren gunner of the Australian 9th Division Infantry covers fellow soldiers as they advance along the railway line on Labuan, flushing out the Japanese occupation forces.

Ultimate weapon unleashed on Japan

An outcome of the Potsdam Agreement was the Potsdam Declaration which set out the terms for Japan's unconditional surrender. These were sent to the Japanese government by Truman, Churchill and China's President Chiang Kai-shek on 26 July. The Japanese government adopted a policy of ignoring the ultimatum because it took away all Japanese sovereignty and reduced its territories as well as threatening the prosecution of war crimes. The response was delivered indirectly by the Japanese Prime Minister in a press conference. The ultimatum was uncompromising in guaranteeing the total devastation of Japan if it did not surrender, but the Imperial forces had no knowledge of the atomic bomb and had already withstood strategic bombing that had destroyed vast areas of some of its cities; the military would rather fight to the death than surrender, leaving the Emperor at the mercy of foreign powers.

Left: The Allied powers called time on the Japanese and sent three B 29 bombers, one of them the *Enola Gay*, equipped with the Little Boy nuclear device to bomb Hiroshima on 6 August, followed by Fat Man dropped on Nagasaki on 9 August. The world suddenly became acquainted with the awesome weapon that would dominate military and political reality for generations to come, symbolised in the terrifying mushroom cloud, photographed here over Nagasaki.

Opposite: Nagasaki razed to the ground.

Hiroshima destroyed

Above: The trio of planes flying towards Hiroshima on 6 August was picked up by Japanese radar and judged to be a reconnaissance flight so no defensive measures were taken. At around 8.15 a.m., the Little Boy nuclear device exploded about 2,000 feet above the target area in central Hiroshima creating a blaze of light and a shock wave that killed an estimated 70,000 citizens instantly and demolished all of the traditionally constructed buildings in range. In the *Enola Gay*, co-pilot Robert Lewis asked the question that would be repeated around the world: 'My God, what have we done?'

Opposite: Directly under the hypocentre was a modern ferro-concrete building which was one of the few that remained standing after the blast. A dazed survivor wanders the scorched streets of Hiroshima. In the months and years to come the survivors continued to die, many of them from terrible burns and horrible radiation sickness.

Tokyo fire-bombed

Opposite: Both Hiroshima and Nagasaki, though they were important cities for military reasons, were relatively untouched by strategic bombing, which enabled the Manhattan Project's researches to continue in 'real' conditions. Tokyo, pictured, was not so unscathed - fire-bombing had already destroyed vast areas of the capital. The Allies avoided fire-bombing Kyoto but many other Japanese cities such as Nagoya were also devastated, fire-bombs destroying the many wooden buildings, rich with Japan's cultural and religious heritage.

Above: On 9 August, as the impact of the two atomic bombs reverberated, the Emperor and his government accepted that surrender was now inevitable; nonetheless they delayed, hoping to retain some vestige of power and dignity. Imperial troops attempted a coup to counter the decision to surrender but on 15 August Japan finally acceded to the terms of the Potsdam Declaration which was then signed by representatives of the Imperial Government and the Allied powers on 2 September aboard USS Missouri anchored in Tokyo Bay. Although the Instrument of Surrender called for an immediate cessation of hostilities, it was not uncommon for Japanese troops to continue resistance and for this reason General Douglas MacArthur insisted that no occupation or release of POWs take place before the official ratification and that the ceremony should be repeated around Japan's main garrisons like Sandakan, Borneo, pictured here on 12 September.

The end is near

Above: Piccadilly Circus in London fills with jubilant crowds on 11 August as news of the crushing blow to Japan filters through.

Opposite: Victory in Japan was made official on 15 August and London came to a standstill as celebrations began in earnest.

By coincidence it was also the State Opening of Parliament and the King and Queen's horse-drawn carriage ride to Westminster turned into an impromptu victory parade. In Trafalgar Square a fountain becomes part of the victory parade!

Living in peace

Opposite: The end of the war brought enormous relief to the many that survived in its shadow but left millions displaced, bereaved, wounded, scarred psychologically or awaiting release from prison - or the serving of a sentence in the courts of justice assembled by the victors. These German POWs fit right into the village life of rural England, forming a choir while they laboured in captivity. Other German prisoners had been transported across the Atlantic to labour for the war effort; many of them were content to stay in the countries that had imprisoned them, knowing the deprivations in their native land.

Above: The rubble of Berlin had to be cleared and the civilians of the city set about creating some order but there was much suffering as the German economy was shattered, the people dazed and afraid of the occupying troops.

Clearing the ruins

Above: The brunt of the Third Reich catastrophe was borne by German men but in the final months and aftermath, women and children shared the hardship of downfall. Here lines of women assist the sorting of bricks and building rubble into re-usable piles in an area of Berlin. The filled pails are passed down the line and their contents sorted.

Opposite: Bomb-scarred but still standing, the American Embassy is to the right of this picture, adjacent to the Brandenburg Gate seen from the side.

Allies Triumph

Opposite: A series of Victory Parades was held in Berlin, the first was a late celebration of VE Day on 6 July, the second, pictured here was a British celebration that paid homage to Winston Churchill and celebrated the endurance of British troops, such as the Desert Rats who saw action in 1940 and marched from the Western Desert to Berlin. Churchill attended the event on 21 July with Field Marshalls Montgomery and Brooke, first inspecting the troops then viewing a parade that drove down the crowded Charlottenburger Chaussee. Here the distinctive Sexton armoured vehicles sporting their 25-pounder guns are immaculately cleaned and painted for the parade. The last of the Victory Parades involved all the Allied forces in a massive marchpast on 7 September.

Right: A key point of the Potsdam Agreement was the trial and conviction of Nazi leaders for crimes against humanity. The international court, in the form of a military tribunal, comprising representatives of all the Allied nations, was set up in Nuremberg at its large Palace of Justice which had survived the war in good condition and had an integrated large jail. Nuremberg, the city which saw the frenzied rallies that initiated the Nazi madness, seemed an appropriate venue to the Allies and 22 of Germany's senior leaders went on trial from 21 November 1945 to 1 October 1946. 12 of the 22 were sentenced to death by hanging; those that remained in custody were executed on 16 October. Göring committed suicide with a cyanide capsule before he could be hanged. In this photograph, an armoured car guards the Palace the day before sentencing.

Nazis sentenced

Above: Sitting in the dock at the Palace of Justice the accused listen to the verdicts as they are read out in English and translated via headphones on 1 October 1946.

Opposite: Rudolf Hess, Hitler's former deputy who tried to broker peace by flying to Britain in 1941, and Joachim von Ribbentrop, Nazi Minister of Foreign Affairs, eat a frugal meal during their trial. Many people in Germany at that time would have been very happy to enjoy such simple fare. Hess had been held in prison since his failed mission and would escape with a life sentence to be served in Spandau Prison; von Ribbentrop was executed.

Night-time celebrations

Opposite: The days following the war were not easy for any of the belligerent nations who began to count the true cost of the nearly six years of cataclysmic warfare. For the Allied nations there was at least a lightness of heart knowing that the conflict was over; for the aggressors, especially Germany and Japan, the crushing of their imperial ambitions gave them the very opposite result they had sought: their people under foreign rule, their flag supplanted and their economy shattered and enslaved to their enemies. The night of VJ Day, 15 August 1945, saw London filled with jubilant crowds, dancing in the street and on the rooftops, lighting bonfires and setting off fireworks.

Above: As soon as the War ended, the majority of troops were able to return to their lives in 'civvy street'. US forces, thousands of miles from home could look forward to their voyage back across the Atlantic or the Pacific and a return to sanity. Here, Sgt Arthur Freund receives his Honourable Discharge, which gave him the thanks of a grateful nation, a substantial cash payment, a service badge for his jacket and his discharge papers. A grand total of 11 million service personnel would follow in his footsteps.

Victory Parade

Left: A grand Victory Parade took place in London on 8 June 1946, bringing together thousands of the servicemen and women who took part in the war. The parade was led by British Chiefs of Staff and the Supreme Allied Commanders; they were followed by over 500 vehicles and a third column of marching troops. The seemingly endless parade stretched for many miles and was topped off with an RAF fly-past. Although all the Allies were invited, Russia, Yugoslavia and Poland were not represented - the decision of the Soviets who had already begun their alienation from their wartime allies in the Western world. The view of the parade in this photograph is from the roof of the Columbia Hotel.

Opposite: The mortal remains of over 4,000 US service personnel were ceremonially carried on board the SS *Lawrence Victory* at Cardiff dock on 16 June 1948, destined for the port of New York City. Most were killed during the D-Day landings and their bodies had to be retrieved from burial locations around France and Germany.

Killed in Action

Many Allied service personnel lay buried close to where they fell, killed in action. Few sights are more stirring and sad than the serried ranks of headstones in the haunted places that mark the heroism of those who gave their lives in the face of inhuman conflict. Here on Iwo Jima, in the US Cemetery of the Fifth Marine Division, lie nearly 7,000 American servicemen who died in the capture of this tiny island that became so symbolic to the world.

At the conclusion of the world's largest conflict, 55 million people, the majority of whom were civilians, lay dead. Around 20 million Russians, 10 million Chinese and 6 million European Jews, who were never part of the 100 million mobilised to fight, are estimated to have perished. In this World War technology increased the death toll by a quantum factor and the conventions of World War II would cast their shadow around the globe for another 50 years or more.

There are voices which assert that the bomb should never have been used at all. I cannot associate myself with such ideas. Six years of total war have convinced most people that had the Germans or Japanese discovered this new weapon, they would have used it upon us to our complete destruction with the utmost alacrity. I am surprised that very worthy people, but people who in most cases had no intention of proceeding to the Japanese front themselves, should adopt the position that rather than throw this bomb, we should have sacrificed a million American, and a quarter of a million British lives in the desperate battles and massacres of an invasion of Japan. Future generations will judge these dire decisions, and I believe that if they find themselves dwelling in a happier world from which war has been banished, and where freedom reigns, they will not condemn those who struggled for their benefit amid the horrors and miseries of this gruesome and ferocious epoch.

Winston S Churchill in his address to Parliament 16 August, 1945